Master Your Mind

11 Mental Hacks to Eliminate Negative Thoughts, Improve Your Emotional Intelligence, and End Procrastination

Master Your Mind

no circumstances is the author responsible for any losses, direct or indirect, which are incurred as a result of the use of information contained within this document, including, but not limited to, — errors, omissions, or inaccuracies.

Table of Contents

Introduction 1

Part One: Take Control of the Way You Think......................... 3

#1 - Goodbye Negativity! Rewiring Your Brain for Positive

Thinking 3

#2 - The Rapid-Fire Guide to Dealing with Stress.................. 9

#3 - How to Move Past Fear and Anxiety............................. 16

#4 - Let Go of the Past and Thoughts That Hold You Back .22

Part Two: The Art of Mastering Emotional Intelligence 26

#5 - Mindfulness: The Art of Becoming Aware of Your

Emotions 26

#6 - How to Communicate Effectively for Better

Relationships 32

#7 - Taking Responsibility for Your Actions 35

#8 - Overcoming Your Limiting Beliefs 37

Part Three: How to Clear Your Life of Procrastination for

Good 41

#9 - How to Zero Down on Difficult Tasks............................ 41

#10 - Developing a Healthy Relationship with Technology . 46

#11 - Would You Rather Score a Goal or Win the Game? 51

Final Thoughts 54

References 55

Introduction

*Life is a game, play it; Life is a challenge, meet it; Life is an opportunity, Capture it. ~ **Unknown***

There are plenty of books out there that talk about how to make your life better. And there's a good chance you already know 99% of the advice they tend to give you.

Usually, such advice falls somewhere along the commonsense lines of; if you want to live an extraordinary life, you need to work hard. Controlling your emotions is important. Otherwise, we'd all be acting on impulse, and the world would be chaos. So many people live their lives riddled with fear and anxiety for multiple reasons. If you want to be happy, positive, and peaceful, you need to work out how to let it all go and move forward.

Sounds simple, right?

While most of the 'self-help' information out there is stuff like this you already know, this book will take a different approach. I'm going to cover some of the most essential topics that will highlight areas of your life that aren't where you want them to be. Those areas that you know deep down are holding you back from being the person you believe you are or at least can be.

However, instead of general advice, this book solely focuses on explaining actionable ways to move past the blockages and obstacles you experience using scientific and psychological actions you can start implementing right here, right now.

That's not to say that change will happen overnight. Oh no. This is going to be a continuous journey, but one where the destination isn't necessary. There is no end goal. This is about having the toolset and skills to have the journey you want. To command your own adventure through your own life. But, that being said, you will see the results almost instantly, and what's great is how exponential and self-perpetuating these results will be.

Before we jump in, a quick note on how this book works, I've divided everything up into three parts. First, we'll start with your mind and address some of the barriers you're living with regarding how you think and perceive yourself and the world.

The second part is all about mastering your emotions - an essential element of your life that will dictate so much of what you do and say and drastically dictate the quality of your life's relationships.

Finally, the third section is about taking action and making your dreams come to fruition through hard work, discipline, and being productive while winning your battles against procrastination and distraction.

So, without further ado, let's get straight into it.

Part One: Take Control of the Way You Think

Whether you think you can or think you can't, you're right. - ***Henry Ford***

#1 - Goodbye Negativity! Rewiring Your Brain for Positive Thinking

Once you replace negative thoughts with positive ones, you'll start having positive results. - ***Willie Nelson***

How often do you have negative thoughts?

According to a National Science Foundation study published in 2005, the average person has between 12,000 and 60,000 thoughts per day. That includes every thought from what you're going to have for lunch to replaying that time you slipped over on a first date 15 years ago.

Of these thoughts, a whopping 80% of these thoughts are harmful, and 95% of these thoughts are repetitive.

Negative thinking is hard-wired into you and every single other being on the planet. It's only natural. Your brain is designed to learn from negative experiences for survival purposes, an instinct that's been genetically in our DNA for hundreds of thousands of years. For example, if you saw your friend get eaten by a Sabre-Toothed Tiger in those woods, you learn from the experience and don't go into those woods. Back then, this way of thinking was a matter of life or death.

From a modern-day perspective, if you touch a hot plate that's just come out of the oven and get burned, you learn the lesson not to touch it again. Then when you see a hot plate, you think of the negative thought to stop you from touching the plate, thus keeping you free from burns and blisters.

On paper, this is a fantastic psychological system to have. Still, it's very outdated for the modern, safe and comfortable world we're living in. Now we get hung up, worried, and stressed about so much more since we have so many more opportunities available. However, our minds still treat the anxiety as life or death.

Let's say you want to be an actor. It's your life-long dream. You go to drama school, and you one day have a bad experience where you forget your lines in one performance.

It was embarrassing, and you felt very ashamed, even though it's an honest mistake that anyone can make. However, you keep replaying the scene in your head over and over again while telling yourself you're worthless because you can't remember your lines. This kind of obsessive negative self-talk then becomes a huge problem.

When this kind of self-talk trumps your positive self-talk, this is the point you'll give up on your dream, and so an unfulfilled life begins. In reality, you forgot your lines in one performance, let's say out of a hundred performances, so statistically, you mess up 1% of the time, which is such a tiny amount and really no reason to give up on your lifelong dream. Yet, this is what so many people do.

You need to highlight the areas of your life where you're thinking negatively about yourself or your life situation and then replace these thoughts with positive thinking!

Let's explore how, but bear in mind this is always an ongoing process. As you move forward in your life and your situation changes, you will need to reapply these steps to address any new negative thoughts.

Step One - Recognize Your Negative Self-Talk

Grab a pen and paper (or a Word document on your computer) and start writing down all the things you dislike about yourself and your life. Literally write down anything and everything that comes to mind and don't worry about spelling or grammar. Of course, take some time to think, but try to write without stopping.

Continue for at least two minutes, but you can write for as long as you want. Here's an excerpt of when I did this exact practice a few years ago.

I hate my diet problems. I binge on junk food, and it's making me fat and unhealthy. I need to quit smoking and stop drinking so much. Some of my friends are bad influences on me. I need to take more responsibility for my actions. I have no drive and ambition. I have no drive and no idea where I want my life to go. I should spend more time outside. I should read more books and practice meditation.

You get the idea. It's not an easy process to go through, but it will open the door to the next step.

Step Two - Identify Your Priorities

It's highly recommended you don't try to change every aspect of your life in one go because it's too much for your mind to cope with. Remember, if your brain could have its way, it would keep you stationary and safe because the fewer problems it has to deal with, the better, but this doesn't make for a fulfilling life.

Instead, highlight two or three of the key areas of your life you want to improve. These can be broad, like saying you want to improve your diet, exercise habits, routines, sleeping pattern, relationship with your partner or children, or you want to work on a project you care about.

Write these priorities down and make them **BOLD**.

Step Three - Turning Negative Talk into Positive Talk

Now you need to take the time to switch around your negative self-talk and turn it into inspiring self-talk that's going to make you want to take action.

This step works by taking what you don't like about yourself and want to improve, and instead of saying you're worthless because you're not where you want to be, you turn these negative thoughts into your foundation on which to grow.

For example, *I binge on junk food, and it's making me fat and unhealthy,* turns into a statement and positive affirmation that reads *I want to practice eating healthy and moderating how much junk food I eat.* As you can see, instead of putting myself down, I'm setting myself up with an actionable goal that's achievable rather than berating myself.

Some rules to remember when approaching this task:

- Write down your positive affirmations every day to drill them into your mind
- Keep practicing. It's not natural for humans to be positive thinkers, and it takes effort!
- Practice not saying anything to yourself that you wouldn't say to other people
- Exaggerate the positive things in your life
- Celebrate the things you do well in your life and succeed at

Keep up with these practices. As your life begins to change, rewrite what you find negative about yourself, prioritize what you want to work on, and go through the process again. It's continuous and ongoing, but the results are life-long.

#2 - The Rapid-Fire Guide to Dealing with Stress

"It's not stress that kills us, it's our reaction to it." – **Hans Selye**

Stress is a massive part of everyone's life that ties in hand in hand with the mental hack above. When you speak to yourself negatively, you're creating stress in your life. If you look at your bank account and fear financial problems occurring in your life, this creates stress. When your partner has a bad day and takes it out on you, this creates stress.

This stress physically sits in your body and causes so many issues. It can make you emotional and irrational, leading you to make unconscious decisions or say things you'll later regret. It can affect your concentration levels, fill you with self-doubt, increase your risk of contracting depression and anxiety, raise your blood pressure, ruin your skin's health, and increase aches and pains in your bones and joints.

In other words, stress isn't good for you. It has a purpose, especially back in the caveman days when the flight or fight response was essential to survival, but nowadays you can get stressed over a passive-aggressive email from your boss. This kind of stress is only going to affect you in an unhealthy way.

The trick to living a happy, unfulfilling, and peaceful life is having the skills to identify when you're stressed. Only then can you take the appropriate actions and decisions to let the stress go, so you're able to refocus and reapply yourself, thus making the decisions you want to make logically and rationally.

So, how do you overcome stress in the first place?

Step One - Identify Stress Triggers in Your Life

You can't fix what you don't know is broken, so start by highlighting areas in your life that you feel stressed about. This requires a degree of knowing yourself and understanding your own physical and mental responses to situations in your life (which takes time and practice). However, I'm going to share the ideas that will help you if you have absolutely no idea where to start, and then you can build off of these techniques in your own way.

Start with thinking about how you feel.

Stress is an essential part of life, but when your stress gets out of control, you're going to feel terrible. If you're frequently feeling anxious, worried, depressed, and have low self-esteem, then yes, you're experiencing stress. If you're feeling exhausted all the time and have problems sleeping, eating, or socializing, then you're experiencing stress. If you get ill often and feel as though that little voice in the back of your head is telling you that something is wrong, then you're feeling stressed.

Of course, you'll feel different degrees of stress at different times in your life. It changes all the time, but being aware that stress is a part of life will help you identify it when it strikes.

Now, just like we did in the first mental hack, take a pen and paper and write down all the things in your life that you think are stressing you out. Don't overthink it, just write down everything that comes to mind. Some ideas that I came up with include:

- My financial situation
- Under a lot of pressure at work
- My partner is horrible to me
- I can't control my children
- I feel that I'm worthless
- I don't have enough work in my life
- I have no goals or direction
- I failed at something I tried to do
- I have a significant change coming up in my life
- I'm ill or sick
- I have lost someone close to me
- I lost my job

Now that you're aware of the problems, you can start focusing on overcoming the stress. This doesn't mean you're going to solve these problems. That's an entirely different ball game that varies from person to person.

However, by alleviating the stress factor, you'll be able to address these problems in a much more grounded, logical way and can therefore be in the best state of mind to deal with them.

Step Two - Relieving Stress and Anxiety

There are endless ways to relieve stress, but the trick is to have the ability to actually do whatever solution helps you, which can vary from person to person. When you're feeling trapped in the clutches of stress, it's easy to think that nothing will help you, so instead, you just sit and let the feelings perpetuate inside you.

Start with a deep breath.

Try this right now for instant proof that this works.

Close your eyes and take a long, deep inhale through your nose with your mouth closed. Inhale for five seconds, ideally for as long as you can, but making sure your lungs are filled all the way to the top.

Now steadily exhale out of your mouth. Try to aim for seven seconds or for as long as you can. Repeat this process three times, then come back.

Five seconds in through the nose. Seven seconds out the mouth. Eyes closed. Repeat three times.

Feels good, doesn't it?

When you're feeling really stressed and don't know what to do, those stressful times when you find yourself completely wrapped up in your own thoughts, go through that process to bring yourself back to a grounded state of mind.

However, while effective and can work any time, it's not a great long-term solution that manages stress over your life.

Exercise frequently.

I can't stress enough how important exercise is for your health and for managing your stress levels.

Science shows that exercise lowers the number of stress hormones in your body (known as cortisol) and releases feel-good hormones like endorphins that make you feel good. This doesn't just work the moment you exercise but has lasting effects that can last for days or even weeks at a time.

Exercise also helps you sleep better, which will dramatically improve the levels of stress in your body. Exercise also makes you more confident in yourself, again reducing stress.

I'm not saying you need to go to the gym. Just go for a ten-minute walk around your local area in a big circle. Just ten minutes in the fresh air will do you a world of good. Personally, I found running works amazingly, but my habits really came into their own when I did just ten minutes of yoga in the morning as soon as I woke up. It's easy. It's light. It takes little effort, but the benefits were huge.

Even just standing up now wherever you are and having a slight stretch for 30 seconds will lower stress in your body. Try it now, feel the effects, and see for yourself how amazing it can feel!

I could go on all day about ways to relieve stress like this, but I'm sure you get the idea. Of course, everyone is different, so here are some other key ways you can alleviate stress:

- Practice mindfulness meditation
- Practice journaling
- Reduce the amount of coffee and alcohol you consume
- Write down what is bothering you at any moment
- Chew chewing gum (this is scientifically proven to work!)
- Socialize with people you love
- Watch something funny and laugh
- Avoid procrastination and distractions
- Listen to music
- Have a bath or shower
- Cook some food
- Practice deep breathing exercises
- Spend time playing with your pets

Step Three - Addressing Your Problems

There's no hard-and-fast way to deal with the problems in your life, but once you're able to get your stress under control, you'll be in the right state of mind to start thinking about how you can do this.

Let's say your financial situation isn't amazing, and you have some credit to pay off. You can get stressed about it, which can lead to substance comfort or comfort spending, or procrastinating to take your mind off your worries, but you never fix the problem.

Instead, by using the methods in the previous step, you alleviate the stress factor, so now you're not running from your problem, but instead are peaceful enough to say, 'okay, how am I going to deal with this?' You could read books on money management, get yourself an advisor, or take on overtime at work to pay your bills.

Whatever the problem is, there's always going to be a solution. This process is the one that will help you find the correct frame of mind to seek it out.

#3 - How to Move Past Fear and Anxiety

Develop success from failures. Discouragement and failure are two of the surest steppingstones to success. - **Dale Carnegie**

One of the most prominent negative thought patterns and emotions you'll experience in your life are those of fear and anxiety. Just as a quick note, that's not referring to the mental health condition of anxiety, but more feelings of the anxiousness you experience day-to-day that can drastically hold you back from living your life to its fullest potential.

For example, imagine you're about to have a job interview for the job of your dreams. Are you excited? Usually a bit, but these days it's extremely common these days to feel more nervous. *What happens if I say the wrong thing? What if I answer a question wrong? What if they don't like me? What if another candidate is better than me? What am I going to do if I don't get this job?*

These are all negative thoughts that can cross your mind, and there are certainly going to be some situations and events in your life where the fearful thoughts are so strong that you won't end up trying something new or taking that risk that could lead to a big step forward for who you as an individual.

Want to write a book? *You can't do that. No one's going to enjoy reading what you write, so I wouldn't even bother.* So, you don't bother even trying to write your book, effectively closing the door on what could be a potentially beautiful part of your life.

This affects every aspect of your life, from the relationships you have, your career, your fitness and health, the experiences you're allowing yourself to have, and so on. You know what I'm talking about. As you read this, thoughts are perhaps popping into your head saying things like, *oh yes, I was scared of this and that and the other.*

Perhaps you regret not being able to move past a fear you've once had, or maybe you're still struggling with it now, no matter how big or small the impact of that fear is.

Fear can manifest in several different ways.

For me, I was fearful of what people would think of me when I started writing these books. I was so scared of public opinions and wouldn't want to be hated if I ever made a mistake or shared a point of view that changed as time went on. This led to me massively procrastinating when I sat down to work on my first book, thus fear was holding me back from doing what I deep-down wanted to spend my life doing.

Of course, there are benefits to fear and anxiety. If you weren't fearful, you'd never stop to think of a logical decision but would instead dive into every situation headfirst without thinking it through. That means you're not being logical or rational, and therefore are unlikely to get the best result possible from any given situation. However, too much fear and anxiety will hold you back and stop you from moving forward.

With the right skills in your toolset, you no longer need to live with these limitations.

Facing Your Fears

The standard advice you'll hear is if you're scared of something, just do it anyway. It's better to do something scared than never to do it at all. Of course, this is precisely what a fearful person doesn't want to hear, and it typically goes over a lot of people's heads, yet, this is a point that needs some perspective.

If you're suffering from fear, the trick isn't to dive in and just face your most significant and boldest fears head-on. Instead, focus on your little fears and practice stepping up to the mark with these. With experience by successfully overcoming your fears in these areas, you'll have the confidence and experience that enable you to face your bigger, more daunting fears.

Let's say you want to ask someone out on a date, but you're fearful of what they'll say. Instead, you can practice facing your fears by talking to strangers whenever you get the opportunity. These are little steps to help you build your experience, so you have the courage to go all the way when it comes to the more important events.

Of course, like the other steps above, this means highlighting what your fears are, so take a pen and paper and write down what you're afraid of and what you fear. Be as comprehensive with your list of fears and see what comes up. You'll be amazed by what patterns appear and how everything ties together, especially when you see how past experiences may have caused you to have a particular fear, but more on that in the next section.

Create Small, Actionable Goals

Now you know what your fears are, you can start working towards overcoming them. However, don't say, *okay, I'm going to write a book from start to finish* because that's way too big and complex. Instead, break your fear down into actionable steps that you can progress through one at a time. In the act of writing a book, your process may look something like this;

- Brainstorm an idea
- Research my idea
- Invent some characters
- Take a writer's class or course
- Write one page
- Write a chapter
- Write the first draft
- Learn about editing

And so on.

If you were fearful of pursuing your dream job, your process broken down into actionable steps could look something like this;

- Identify what my dream job is
- Identify what skills and qualifications I need to get there
- What courses, skills, and tests do I need to do?
- How much education and experience do I need?
- What time frame am I looking at if I start now?
- When can I start?
- How do I apply for jobs?
- What are companies looking for?
- Are there apprenticeship programs?
- Can I work my way up in the company?

As you can see, instead of just dropping yourself in this massively complex idea of doing something with your life, which is going to be big and scary, you're taking little steps at a time, which will eventually lead to big results. Make sure your steps are manageable, so you can set them as goals. The human mind works so much more effectively when it has a clear and concise goal to work towards.

Highlight Your Excuses
When you're scared of doing something, it's easy to make excuses, and when you listen and agree with such

thoughts, it means the fear has won. You've developed a reason for the fear to hold you back. You need to be active in recognizing your excuses, as and when they come up and then providing yourself with alternative thoughts to think.

Think of the classic excuse as to why you won't do something. The classic *I'm too tired. I'll do it tomorrow.* Think critically of yourself. Are you too tired, or are you just saying that because you're lazy or scared? If you're scared or lazy, then recognize you're making an excuse and go back to the previous step and start working on a small step that can take you forwards towards completing your bigger picture.

If you are genuinely tired, then you know it's time to work on adjusting your sleeping pattern to make sure you're well-rested and looking after yourself properly. This way, you can give yourself the time and energy to work on the things you want to work on.

#4 - Let Go of the Past and Thoughts That Hold You Back

Holding on is believing that there's a past; letting go is knowing that there's a future. -Daphne Rose Kingma

Part One wouldn't be complete without taking a look at the negative thought patterns, feelings, and emotions that we all have and perhaps experience more often than we'd like to admit, and that is your past coming up and haunting your present.

Numerous problems come from holding onto the past. Firstly, it ruins your present moment. You can't fully appreciate and feel grateful for what's in front of you if you're too busy focusing on the past, especially since it's typically going to be mistakes you've made or bad things that have happened to you. Again, this is entirely normal, and everyone feels this way since the mind is designed to remember the bad times in an attempt to protect you and survive moving forward, but it's an old instinct out of touch with the safety and comfort of the modern world.

Now, since this is how your brain is literally designed to work, you're not going to stop the bad, negative thoughts from occurring, nor can you clear your mind from thinking completely. However, you can learn to instead break the cycle by letting go of the emotions connected to your past thoughts and feelings, the same emotional ties that are holding you back right now.

For example, let's say you've been through a bad breakup that was messy and scarred you. It left you feeling like you're not worth anything, and since your partner cheated on you, you feel as though you weren't good enough. These feelings can give you trust issues in your future relationships and may stop you from even trying new relationships altogether.

If you're finding yourself entering relationships and seemingly unintentionally self-sabotaging them, this could well and truly be what you're going through. Your mind is sabotaging the relationship through you to stop you from being hurt again.

This logic, of course, applies to any area of your life. Perhaps you did the cheating, or you screwed over and hurt someone else. Maybe you made a mistake, and you can't let it go. Either way, it's time to reframe your connection with your own past self.

Accepting the Past for What It Is

If something terrible has happened in your past, you may try and be the hero of your own story by creating a false version of it. You may blame someone or something else for a mistake you made because you don't want to make it seem as though you're weak, embarrassed, nor admit that you messed up.

You must take responsibility for your actions, and yes, while there are things in life outside of your control, there are many things that are. Remember that everyone hurts other people, and everyone makes mistakes. It's all a part of life and the learning process. You need to make peace that what has happened has happened, and it's fine just the way it is.

Then you can take onboard your lesson that you've learned and apply the teachings to present and future self.

Your Problems are Not You

There's a bit of an epidemic going around at the moment that so many people take their problems into themselves and allow it to define who they are. You probably know or have known someone that drinks a lot too much, more than what is healthy, but they make this problem a part of who they are, perhaps identifying themselves as the fun-loving free one of the friend group.

It's this kind of mentality that makes it hard for people to let go of their problems because it's part of who they are, and nobody wants that part of them taken away, because if it is, who is left in their place after it's gone?

The best thing to remember here is that your story shapes and guides who you are as a person, but they don't create the person you are right now. You could completely change your life right now if you really wanted to, and your past can't do a thing about that.

Understanding this power, well, makes you a powerful and potential-filled individual.

Forgive Yourself

You make mistakes. I make mistakes. We've all hurt people and done things we'd probably do differently if given a chance. It's a part of life, and you need to learn to forgive yourself. You know situations in your own life where people have hurt you or done something wrong, perhaps a friend or a partner, and they've apologized, you've accepted it, and everyone moves on? You need to be able to do that to yourself.

Errors can always be set right, and we can always learn lessons from the things we do wrong. The life-changing advice here is understanding that you're allowed to forgive yourself and move on, and you don't have to hold yourself back because you messed up once a long time ago.

Part Two: The Art of Mastering Emotional Intelligence

#5 - Mindfulness: The Art of Becoming Aware of Your Emotions

When our emotional health is in a bad state, so is our level of self-esteem. We have to slow down and deal with what is troubling us, so that we can enjoy the simple joy of being happy and at peace with ourselves.
-Jess C. Scott

Emotional intelligence is a vital part of living a happy and fulfilled life. As I described in the introduction, imagine if you went through life just reacting to every single emotion that came up in any situation. If someone made you upset, you'd shout and scream at them, potentially even physically hurting them, all because they annoyed you, even if it was only a tiny little thing that happened in the first place.

While everybody has some degree of emotional intelligence, but otherwise the world would be in absolute chaos, there are certainly times we could be even more intelligent, and this would solve a lot of problems in your life.

For example, when you're talking to your partner and they say something triggering. The chances are you feel the defensiveness creep into your replies. You feel stiff and threatened. You physically feel angered and as though you want to defend your point of view. You start to raise your voice and become passive-aggressive in what you say.

At this point, you're not in control of your emotions. Your emotions are in control of you, and this is the state of mind where you'll potentially say something to hurt your partner, or you'll say something out of emotion that you'll later regret. Maybe you've completely lost your temper with someone, and you've acted out of pure emotion before, and you already know the consequences of losing your cool in such a way can be incredibly damaging to any relationship or reputation.

This might all sound slightly complicated and a lot to take in, but let's break it down to the basics. The first skill to learn is all about being able to spot your emotions coming up in the first place. If you're able to spot an emotion building up inside you, it means you've already taken a moment to pause and check-in with yourself. This gives you the chance to decide how you're really feeling and then how you choose to respond, rather than just proceeding on your mindless auto-pilot setting.

Increasing Your Self Awareness
Start small.

As you go through your day, start paying attention to how you feel and the emotions you're experiencing in any given situation. Ask yourself how you're feeling right now. Are you happy, sad, content, stressed, tired, angry, irritated, bored, and so on? Now ask yourself how these emotions physically feel within your body. If you're nervous or fearful, for example, you may feel sweaty and slightly nauseous.

The more you practice this, the better and more consistent at it you'll become. This means you'll be more aware of how you feel when someone cuts you up in traffic. Say someone cuts you off and forces you to hard brake, you may automatically start shouting at and cursing that other person. However, with this kind of practice, you'll instead notice the feelings of anger and irritation rising up.

Now how are you going to respond? Sure, if you want to curse the driver and shout at him, go ahead. At least you're choosing to be this way. On the other hand, you may choose to take a deep breath and let it go. It happened. It's done. It's in the past. It's not really a problem. Let it go. Now you don't have to take onboard that anger and irritation that will clearly ruin the rest of your day, and you can move forward content and at peace.

This is far better for your health and your overall happiness!

Identify Your Triggers

Everyone has a trigger of some kind, and it can be worth taking the time to explore what your own are, so you're mindful of what you need to be on the lookout for. An excellent place to start is in your past, looking at your own life experiences that will explain why you think and feel the way you do.

For example, if you've been cheated on in the past. You may have trust issues and when your current partner says they're going to hang out with a friend of the opposite sex, you feel triggered. Feelings of jealousy, clinginess, and obsessiveness start to creep in. In a normal situation, these feelings may mindlessly control you to constantly message your partner to get them checking in with you, stalking their social media feeds, or having panic attacks because you feel as though you're going to be cheated on.

However, since you've identified you have a trust issue, you know that the way you're feeling is perfectly valid and something you're working on. You don't need to react mindlessly, but instead say, *'Oh, here's the issue I've been dealing with. Now I can take actions to calm myself down and remain in control.'*

In this situation, you'll remain calm and collected, which over time will allow you to let go of your trust issues. Eventually, you won't have to deal with the trigger at all, which is a much more beneficial approach for your happiness and the peacefulness in your relationship.

Be Compassionate and Empathy

As you start to become more aware of your emotions and thought patterns, like the negative ones we discussed in Part One, it's only natural that you're going to start to judge yourself. You may even condemn yourself for having negative thoughts all the time or thinking and feeling the way you do. You might think, *'Why am I feeling this way? It's unhealthy to feel this way, and I shouldn't be feeling like this.'*

This is how your negative thoughts have now adapted from the negative thoughts at the beginning to now judging yourself, and thus they can continue to exist. Again, this is your mind trying to control you and keep you safe while living in the modern world.

The very best way to deal with this is to have compassion and empathy for yourself, which of course extends to others as well. Everyone, including you, is just a human being trying their best to do what they think is right with the best of what they have. Adopting this mindset can help you release judgments from yourself, thus finding more peace.

You might notice you have a negative emotion rise up, and you think *'Oh, there's a negative emotion.'* Then you might be mad at yourself for having the negative emotion. Just remember that every feeling, emotion, and thought you have can teach you something about yourself, and noticing them arise makes you far more of a well-rounded and grounded individual than most other people will ever be in their entire lives. It's an incredibly peaceful and fulfilling way to live your life that will bring endless benefits.

Practice Mindfulness

I left this point until the end because many people have dubious opinions about what mindfulness and meditation practices are, which can be off-putting. While understandable, everything we've spoken about already is a form of being mindful. You can take this so much further by actively practicing meditation daily.

Sure, sitting on the floor still and silently for ten minutes a day is not everyone's cup of tea, and that's fine. If it's not for you, it's not for you. However, give it a try for a week (just ten minutes per day), perhaps using an app or YouTube video to guide you. You will start to notice benefits in your life when it comes to your ability to spot and identify your emotions which will only contribute to you becoming a more emotionally intelligent individual. If you haven't tried it before, then it's well worth checking out!

#6 - How to Communicate Effectively for Better Relationships

Communication to a relationship is like oxygen to life. Without it... it dies. - **Tony Gaskins**

Once you've started paying attention to your emotions, you'll start to notice that your interactions with the world will already start improving. Whereas you may have previously been saying things you regret to your partner, parents, or friends that make some situations worse, now you're communicating in a much more grounded and compassionate way, but now we can continue to take things a bit further.

Being emotionally intelligent in a relationship with anybody in your life means communicating with them properly. This specific life hack is all about everything encompassed within this topic with the goal of being able to develop meaningful and fulfilling relationships with the people in your life, all via how you communicate with them.

Learn to Listen

The bread-and-butter tip when it comes to bettering how you communicate.

How often do you have a conversation with someone, and either you or they feel like you're just waiting for the other person to finish talking so you can say whatever it is you wanted to say? That's not having a proper conversation, but rather just waiting for your turn to speak. How can you possibly understand someone and what they're telling you if you're just waiting for your turn?

To be a better communicator, learn to leave everything you want to say at the door and instead spend that energy on listening to what someone is saying and trying to understand them to the best of your ability.

Ask Questions

This may sound like a silly point, but if you don't know something or you're not entirely sure about what someone is saying, or the meaning behind what they're saying, then don't be afraid to ask questions. If you do this already, then great, keep it up. However, there will almost certainly be people in your life where they say something, and you don't want to look silly or naive, so you stay quiet and pretend you know what they're talking about.

Again, you're not going to develop a relationship with them if you're not understanding them correctly, so drop your ego and ask for clarity!

Be Emotionally Intelligent

Tying in everything we've already spoken about in this Part, bring your skills of emotional intelligence into your conversations by highlighting the emotions that someone else is feeling and then adjusting your reactions accordingly. If someone is defensive or passive-aggressive towards you, then you're probably right in thinking that you've said something to trigger them, to which you can validate them by saying something like;

"I'm sorry. I didn't mean what I said in a way to offend you. What I meant was..." and so on. This will make the other person feel as though you really understand how they feel, and they will be far more likely to continue having a productive conversation with you.

#7 - Taking Responsibility for Your Actions

"The price of greatness is responsibility."– **Winston Churchill James**

It's hard to take responsibility for your actions. As I said above, nobody wants to own up to their mistakes really because it can make you feel weak and as though you're a lousy human being, but if you're unable to take responsibilities for your own actions, you'll never be able to grow and become the best version of yourself. Rather, you'll just stay where you are.

If you feel like a victim because life is against you and holding you back, or you feel as though people in your life are out to screw you and will try to win one over on you, you're never going to get anywhere. Yes, bad things will happen to you, and yes, people will take advantage, but you always have control over yourself and the decisions you make and have made. Taking ownership of this will bring so much power into your life.

Some of the best ways to take ownership and responsibility for your actions include:

- Not blaming other people for things
- Paying attention to what you complain about
- Highlighting the excuses you create for situations in your life

- Setting goals that you can actionably aim towards fulfilling
- Learning how to love yourself
- Being responsible for your physical and mental health
- Accepting that you will always have to deal with negative emotions and beliefs
- Understanding you will make mistakes in life
- Understanding that your actions and what you say are always in your control
- Your emotional intelligence is your responsibility

#8 - Overcoming Your Limiting Beliefs

"You begin to fly when you let go of self-limiting beliefs and allow your mind and aspirations to rise to greater heights." —**Brian Tracy**.

Limiting beliefs are the thought patterns in your life that repeatedly appear, usually without you really realizing it, that hold you back from doing what you want. I used to love the idea of being a person of habit. I wanted to exercise regularly and have a proper sleeping pattern. I wanted to watch less TV and spend less time playing video games and work on projects that actually benefited my life.

However, I saw people who were successful in these ways and believed myself not to be anything like them. I used to vow every weekend that the new me would start on Monday, and by the end of the week, I'd be back to my old habits. What gives? What beliefs stopped me from just doing what I wanted to do? It was frustrating for so many years. It wasn't until I started practicing emotional intelligence that I could figure out what these beliefs were and eventually overcome them.

It turns out that many of your beliefs are set before the age of seven. A classic example is a child singing at home when their mother gets home from work. The mother has a bad day and a massive headache, and hearing the child singing, she says, 'can you please stop that noise? You're giving me a headache.

Even though the child has the voice of an angel, they believe that their singing is bad and causes headaches, and therefore develops the belief that they should never sing again. This belief continues through to when the child is an adult, and they may sing once, and someone will say, wow, your voice is incredible, to which that same person doesn't believe this to be the case, thus they have a limiting belief.

How do you overcome them?

Again, you need to start using your emotional intelligence.

Start by paying attention to how you think and feel. When do you say things like 'I can't...', 'I am a...', 'I'm not able to...', 'I don't have the...", and so on. Try writing them down now and see what you come up with.

A fascinating exercise I love to try with people is getting them to write down the ideal amount for how much they'd love to earn realistically. Averagely, people say around $50,000. Whatever your own figure, add a zero to the end. $500,000 a year. Now write down all the reasons you can think of as to why you can't earn this amount.

These are your limiting beliefs when it comes to your finances. You can repeat this process for literally any aspect of your life, as many times as you want!

Moving Past Your Limiting Beliefs

Now that you've identified your limiting beliefs, you can start working on overcoming them. Start by asking yourself whether your belief is actually true or not. Some beliefs you'll write down and look back at, and it can be hard to laugh to think that it's a belief you actually thought you believed. These are easy beliefs to let go of.

For me, I thought people didn't care about me and I gave the example that nobody reaches out for me on my birthday, especially since I don't have a personal Facebook page. But then I looked back, and people did reach out to me. One even said they wished they knew earlier so they could have organized something nice to do. In this situation, this limiting belief simply wasn't true.

However, there will be beliefs that you believe are solidly true. For example, you might think you can't have your dream job because you're smart enough to be educated and therefore will never be qualified to do it. You need to take these beliefs and replace them with alternative beliefs.

A great way to do this is by imagining a friend telling you that they don't believe they're educated enough for their dream job, then giving them the advice you would give them, and then onboarding this advice yourself. Consider what type of goals a person should set to get to where they want to be, then use these ideas to replace existing beliefs with actionable goals (broken down into small, manageable steps) that will take them in the direction you want to go. Then heed your own advice.

Part Three: How to Clear Your Life of Procrastination for Good

#9 - How to Zero Down on Difficult Tasks

It is our attitude at the beginning of a difficult task which, more than anything else, will affect its successful outcome. - **William James.**

A lot of this book so far has been talking about identifying where you are now as an individual and taking stock of what's going on in your life and in your head, but it almost always leads back to you having to create goals and take action that will lead you forward in your life.

But this isn't always easy. In fact, 99% of the time, it's hard work.

Whether you're breaking old habits in favor of new ones or working towards a goal, like bettering your relationship, securing your dream job, working on your mental health, or sorting out your financial situation. Along this process, there are always going to be things you don't want to do and difficult tasks, and if there were a way to enjoy doing them, it would make the journey so much better and more inviting.

Fortunately, there are—several ways actually, which is precisely what we're exploring in this hack. I'm going to assume you already know what part of the task you find difficult, but it could also be the tasks you find boring, frustrating, annoying, challenging, lacking in fulfillment, and so on. Here's how to make them more enjoyable.

What is the Hard Part?

First, start with highlighting what the hard part of your task is. What are you struggling with? The chances are that out of a big life goal, there are only one or two parts that are actually different that end up tainting the rest. The entire process will rarely be completely difficult from start to finish.

Once you've highlighted the hard bit, you can start spending your time on the aspects you can do while figuring out ways you can approach the harder areas of concern.

Breaking the Task Down

Hand in hand with the point above, it's always worth breaking the task down into manageable sections, just like we've spoken about in this book already. Instead of saying 'I want to be financially secure,' which is a massive, unspecific goal, you would break this down into parts like:

- I need to earn $2,000 per month

- Which is $500 per week.
- Which is $100 per working day
- Which is $12 per hour
- I need to find a job that pays $15 per hour that's 40 hours per week to earn $600
- Find a job like this and use the extra $400 per month to pay off my credit card

And so on. Breaking the task down, even big, ambitious goals, will help it become more manageable and approachable.

Find Tools to Help

We live in the modern world where there are plenty of tools out there to help you complete whatever task you want to set your mind to. Want to manage your finances? Use a spreadsheet or money management software. Need to manage your time better and schedule? Start using a calendar. Struggling with your mental health? Start seeing a professional.

Remember, no matter what you're going through or trying to achieve in your life, there are tools, people, and resources out there to help you get it done. You never have to just struggle to try to figure things out by yourself.

Start with the Easy Bit

You'll often find yourself procrastinating because you don't want to deal with the challenging aspects of the task, and therefore won't start it because it's not worth coming up against that obstacle. However, it doesn't matter what you're working on. There's always going to be something you can do.

Since there's always an aspect of the task that can be completed, so when the difficulty sets in and the urges to procrastinate begin, use your broken-down task and start working on an easy bit that you can manage. The best thing you can do when facing a problem is to start somewhere, and that really doesn't matter where, because once you get started, your mind will start focusing on possible solutions to your problems.

Be Clear on Your Final Goal

Always keep your final goal in mind, and this will help get you through the hardest parts of your task.

Let's say you're working a big overtime shift, and you're struggling and feeling miserable. When you picture what financial freedom would look like, this can be all you need to inspire yourself to keep going. Whether having a challenging conversation with your partner or going for a run, picture the end goal in mind to motivate yourself to keep going.

You can level this point up by actually sitting down and writing out your end goal and what you're aiming for. What does your life look like when the task is successfully completed? If you're really struggling and need the motivation, take the time to write out what your life would look like if you didn't complete the task and how that would feel.

By visualizing your life in this way, you can seriously motivate yourself to get things done.

#10 - Developing a Healthy Relationship with Technology

*"All of our technology is completely unnecessary to a happy life."— **Tom Hodgkinso***

There's no denying that technology will play a huge role in your procrastination efforts. How often have you been trying to do something, and you've suddenly, sometimes without warning, found yourself deep in your Instagram Explore feed, scrolling through Instagram or Facebook stories, on a YouTube binge, and so on?

It's an attention epidemic, and your attention span is being destroyed by the pull of these apps and services that are designed to keep you hooked as long as possible. However, this is incredibly destructive to your life. The average 30-something in 2019 spends around 144 minutes on social media per day. That's just social media. That doesn't include answering text messages, making phone calls, emails, browsing other blogs and websites, playing games, and so on, so you can expect that time to be much higher.

Let's say your time is worth $20 per hour (not including the extra time you spend on your phone as you wake up and before you go to bed, as well as more time at the weekends or whenever you're not working). This means you're missing out on around $14,560 per year, just on social media. Ouch.

Being in control of how you use technology (or how technology uses you) is essential to your peace, happiness, and fulfillment in life, and without a healthy relationship with technology, you're going to continuously find yourself procrastinating and being stuck where you are over and over again. Here are some actionable tips you can use to start managing your relationship more effectively.

See Where You're At

You can easily track how much you're spending on your devices with a bit of mindfulness. Try to write down every day how much time you're spending at your computer, on your phone, and watching TV. It doesn't matter whether you have an Android phone or tablet or an Apple device; they have software built into the gadgets that allow you to see how much time you're spending on them.

Fair warning, the number is probably going to be more shocking than you think. This is important, however, because it will show you the reality of your situation, and if you're working out how much time and money you're wasting, it can be a significant source of motivation to want to make a change.

Turn Off Notifications

Now, the very best way to curb your digital usage is by turning off all notifications from your devices, except those that you absolutely need. Notifications exist to draw you back into using a device. That's why Facebook will randomly notify you out of the blue that some random person has uploaded a photo or posted something. It's trying to draw you back in because once you're back on the app, the chances are you're going to stay there for a longer period of time.

Turning off your notifications and getting into the habit of checking your devices for messages and so on at set times of the day can be a great way to curb impulsive device usage and instead promotes a healthy habit where you are in control, not just lured in by the pings and dings you're used to.

Remove Your Device from View

When you've got your device in your pocket the entire time, in your hand, or next to you on your sofa, table, or desk, then of course it's going to be hard to ignore it, especially when your brain wants to dive into the content to see what's going on online.

A great way to stop this from happening is simply leaving your device in another room and only going to it during set times of the day. This has been especially important for me because I work from home and having my phone on my desk just makes me want to go on it all the time. However, if I leave it in my kitchen, I only check and interact with it while waiting for the kettle to boil, limiting the amount of time I'm online and helping me to focus on what I actually need to be working on.

Use a Tool or Service

Whether you're managing your time on your phone or computer, there are tools out there to help. iOS devices, for example, have ScreenTime built into the phone that you can say you want to use your phone for no longer than an hour per day and will need to go through unlocking the device with a code if you want entry after this time. It's not hard to remove the block, but the extra steps act as a great reminder that stops you from just opening and going on your phone mindlessly.

The same applies to desktop computers and laptops. It can be so easy just to find yourself on websites prone to procrastinators, so install a website blocker that can block your crutch websites for a set amount of time while you're working. These tools are here to help, so use them!

There are other things to do that can help you with your relationship with technology, not just to stop you procrastinating, but also to better your mental health, and overall just keep you a bit saner while spending time online, specifically on social media.

- Curate your feeds and unfollow content you don't care about
- Steer clear of online toxic behavior and trends (it will only make you unhappy)

- Start a schedule that allows you to use your devices during set hours of the day only
- Be positive online and share positive content that benefits the lives of others

#11 - Would You Rather Score a Goal or Win the Game?

"To lose patience is to lose the battle." – **Mahatma Gandhi**.

Finally, to conclude this short little punchy book (which has been a joy to write, and I hope you've enjoyed it too), I want to talk about patience. No matter what you're doing in your life, whether you're working on an aspect of this book, working towards a goal or setting yourself a project, working on yourself, or just trying to do anything in life, remember that you need patience.

There's a big difference between the happiness and fulfilment you'll get from chasing short-term pleasures and achieving long-term goals. It's the difference between scoring a single goal in a football match and winning the championship. Long-term, you get to play ball with games like legacy, life-long dream fulfillment, and discovery of yourself.

Short-term pleasures come in the form of masturbating excessively (research shows that Pornhub alone receives over 64 million users a day, clocking up over 90 billion views), eating an entire pizza to yourself, watching one more episode of the series you're binging, or chasing someone as a partner you know isn't right for you, but you find them to be very attractive.

I use such graphic examples because it's literally the kind of short-term goals so many find themselves chasing but spending their energy on these goals prevents them from having any drive to pursue their long-term ones, and so they get left by the wayside.

Fast forward to the later years of someone's life, they'll look back at the short-term pleasures that no longer serve them nor bring them happiness, and wonder what happened to all the dreams and ambitions they had. I'm not saying you shouldn't enjoy short-term pleasures. There's obvious joy there as long as you're responsible and sticking to your values. However, real-life satisfaction comes from chasing long-term goals, and this requires patience while you work hard and wait for the results to come.

Here are some tips you may find that help:

- Be mindful of your impatience. If you feel like you're stopping work on your long-term goals to chase a short-term one, become aware of the urge and the pull to the short-term goal, and decide whether it's something you want to pursue.

- Figure out your triggers. We all have triggers that make us impatient from time to time. Perhaps you're working towards a goal, head over to social media, and see someone else who is already where you want to be and makes you feel bad about your situation. Instead, recognize this is a trigger and minimize your exposure to them.

- Be confident in yourself. There are dozens of ways to crack a nut, so be confident in your own journey and that the steps you're taking, no matter what you're working on, will take you to where you want to go. It may take a bit longer, or it may be faster than other people's journey, but that's okay. Enjoy your journey because you're the only one who gets to walk it.

- Visualize the worst-case scenario. When you're impatient, perhaps surprisingly, it's when things are going well, but you're craving for them to be better. When you're stressed out and things are bad, you're too busy trying to solve problems, and so impatience doesn't even come to mind. When things are good, and you're feeling impatient, try to picture in your mind how bad things could be in your life right here, right now.

It's this degree of gratitude and appreciation that can ground you and make you fulfilled with where you are right now on your journey.

Final Thoughts

And so, we come to the end of our journey.

I hope you've enjoyed the ride as much as I've enjoyed creating it! By following through these mental hacks and focusing on these specific areas of your life, you can bring about such incredible, such awe-inspiring change in the areas of your life that you want to work on.

While some people believe it's belittling to always be seeking out ways to change ourselves, that's not at all the case. Instead, self-development in the ways we've discussed is a never-ending journey to better ourselves as individuals, not in a way that you're unhappy the way your life is now (although this is certainly a motive to want to make change), but rather a chance for you to grow and live the life you *want* to live.

If you let it, your mind will always play against what you want if you're running on autopilot because it's easier just to stay where you are. However, with the right tools in your toolbox, the right skills, and a conscious mindset where the true you takes control, you can live whatever life you want to live, so good luck on your journey, and I'll see you soon!

References

Negative Self-Talk: Don't Let It Overwhelm You. (2021). Retrieved 8 April 2021, from https://www.psychologytoday.com/us/blog/family-affair/201712/negative-self-talk-dont-let-it-overwhelm-you

How Stress Affects Us. (2021). Retrieved 8 April 2021, from https://www.stress.org.uk/how-it-affects-us/

Causes of stress. (2021). Retrieved 8 April 2021, from https://www.mind.org.uk/information-support/types-of-mental-health-problems/stress/causes-of-stress/

16 Simple Ways to Relieve Stress and Anxiety. (2021). Retrieved 8 April 2021, from https://www.healthline.com/nutrition/16-ways-relieve-stress-anxiety#16.-Spend-time-with-your-pet

How to Let Go of the Past. (2021). Retrieved 8 April 2021, from https://www.psychologytoday.com/us/blog/the-adaptive-mind/202002/how-let-go-the-past

Brooks, S. (2021). 5 ways to make communication more effective. Retrieved 8 April 2021, from https://blog.ttisi.com/5-ways-make-communication-effective

How To Use The Power Of Visualization To Create A New Reality. (2021). Retrieved 8 April 2021, from https://blog.mindvalley.com/the-power-of-visualization/

7 Brilliant Tips to Handle The Hard Tasks. (2021). Retrieved 8 April 2021, from https://www.lifehack.org/articles/productivity/7-brilliant-tips-handle-the-hard-tasks.html

Happy, G., Chernoff, M., Ham, W., Shirvanian, A., Tompkins, H., & Lee, T. et al. (2021). How To Make Difficult Tasks Easier. Retrieved 8 April 2021, from https://www.marcandangel.com/2009/10/05/how-to-make-difficult-tasks-easier/

6 Steps For Setting Clear Goals You Can Realistically Achieve. (2021). Retrieved 8 April 2021, from https://www.diygenius.com/setting-clear-goals/

Before you continue to YouTube. (2021). Retrieved 8 April 2021, from https://www.youtube.com/watch?v=z3TJPyHqadY

James W. Williams